Choirs of Angels
Coloring Book

With Quotes from the Bible

Illustrated by Katherine Sotnik

HOLY IMITATION® series

IGNATIUS PRESS   SAN FRANCISCO

This book is dedicated in honor of our guardian angels

The artist gratefully acknowledges the permission granted to use the line drawing on page CA44, based on the original painting *The Annunciation to Mary* (Rec. 8678), courtesy of the Ricci Institute for Chinese-Western Cultural History at the University of San Francisco Center for the Pacific Rim.

Scripture verses have been taken from the Revised Standard Version of the Holy Bible, Catholic Edition. The Revised Standard Version of the Holy Bible: the Old Testament, © 1952; the Apocrypha, © 1957; the New Testament, © 1946; the Catholic Edition of the Old Testament, incorporating the Apocrypha, © 1966; the Catholic Edition of the New Testament, © 1965, by the Division of Christian Education of the National Council of the Churches of Christ in the United States of America. All rights reserved.

The linework was rendered with technical ink pens on vellum, and with a digitizer pen and tablet.

Published in 2012 by Ignatius Press, San Francisco
ISBN 978-1-58617-588-7
Manufactured by Thomson-Shore, Dexter, MI (USA); RMA579LS497, January, 2012

Let the heavens praise thy wonders,
O Lᴏʀᴅ, thy faithfulness in the
assembly of the holy ones!

Ps 89:5

CA3

Music-Making Angels (detail) by Melozzo da Forli

Praise the Lord! Praise the Lord from the heavens, praise him in the heights!

Angel (detail) from the *Coronation of the Virgin* by Raphael Sanzio da Urbino

Praise him, all his angels,
praise him, all his host!

Praise him, sun and moon,
praise him, all you shining stars!

CA7

Ps 148:5

Let them praise the name of the LORD!
For he commanded
and they were created.

Make a joyful noise to the LORD, all the earth; break forth into joyous song and sing praises!

Ps 98:4   CA8   *Virgin of the Swaddling Clothes* by Bartolomé Esteban Murillo

Bless the Lord, O you his angels,
you mighty ones who do his word,
hearkening to the voice of his word!

Then I saw the seven angels who stand before God, and seven trumpets were given to them.

Rev 8:2

Angel playing a trumpet (detail) from the Linaiuoli Tabernacle by Fra Angelico

Coronation of the Virgin (detail) by Fra Angelico

Now the seven angels who
had the seven trumpets
made ready to blow them.

Above him stood the seraphim;
each had six wings...

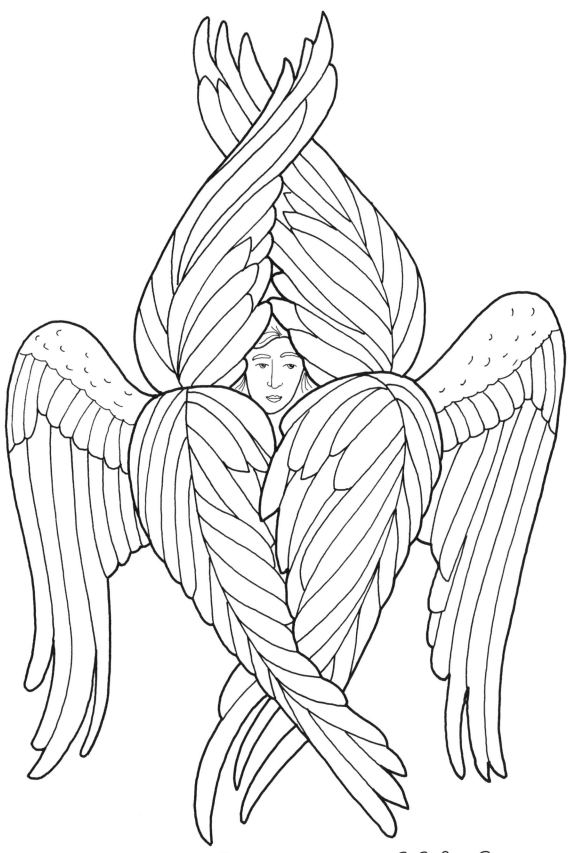

...with two he covered his face,
and with two he covered his feet,
and with two he flew.

And the sound of the wings of the cherubim was heard as far as the outer court, like the voice of God Almighty...

Based on *Angel with Flute* by Raphael Sanzio da Urbino

Ezek 10:5   CA14

Thou who art enthroned upon the cherubim, shine forth...

And all the angels stood round the
throne and round the elders
and the four living creatures...

"Holy, holy, holy,
is the Lord God Almighty,
who was and is and is to come!"

"Just so, I tell you, there is joy before the angels of God over one sinner who repents."

Angel with a drum (detail) from the Linaiuoli Tabernacle by Fra Angelico

Angel with a violin (detail) from the Linaiuoli Tabernacle by Fra Angelico

CA19

Eph 3:10

...the manifold wisdom of God might now be made known to the principalities and powers in the heavenly places.

"Father, if thou art willing, remove this cup from me; nevertheless not my will, but thine, be done."

CA20

The Prayer in the Garden (detail) by Lorenzo Ghiberti

And there appeared to him
an angel from heaven,
strengthening him.

"O Lᴏʀᴅ the God of Israel, who art
enthroned above the cherubim,
thou art the God, thou alone..."

2 Kings 19:15   CA22   *The Assumption of Mary by Taddeo di Bartoli*

For the Son of man is to come with his angels in the glory of his Father, and then he will repay every man for what he has done.

"Praise him with trumpet sound; praise him with lute and harp! Praise him with timbrel and dance; praise him with strings and pipe!"

Ps 150:3-4 CA24 Two angels with instruments by Gherardo Starnina

Angel with a tambourine (detail) from the Linaiuoli Tabernacle by Fra Angelico

Col 1:16

...whether thrones or dominions or principalities or authorities — all things were created through him and for him.

"...there is none who contends by my side against these except Michael, your prince."

Archangel Raphael by Bartolomé Esteban Murillo

"I am Raphael, one of the seven holy angels who present the prayers of the saints..."

"At that time shall arise Michael, the great prince who has charge of your people."

Dan 12:1   CA28   *Justice Between the Archangels* by Jacobello Del Fiore

...the archangel Michael, contending with the devil...said, "The Lord rebuke you."

The Resurrection (angel detail) by Passignano (also known as Domenico Cresti)

CA30

Lk 24:4

While they were perplexed about this,
behold, two men stood by them
in dazzling apparel...

The Resurrection (angel detail) by Passignano

Lk 24:5

...and as they were frightened and bowed their faces to the ground, the men said to them...

ΌΡ ΜΙ   ΧΑΗΛ   ΌΡ ΓΑ   ΒΡΙΗΛ

"Why do you seek the living among the dead? He is not here, but has risen."

"Remember how he told you...that the Son of man must be...crucified, and on the third day rise."

In the sixth month the angel Gabriel was sent from God to a city of Galilee named Nazareth...

The Annunciation (angel detail) by Fra Angelico

The Annunciation by Fra Angelico

...to a virgin betrothed to a man whose name was Joseph, of the house of David; and the virgin's name was Mary.

And he came to her and said, "Hail, full of grace, the Lord is with you!"

CA36   *The Annunciation* (angel detail) by Fra Angelico

The Annunciation (Mary detail) by Fra Angelico

But she was greatly troubled at the saying, and considered in her mind what sort of greeting this might be.

And the angel said to her, "Do not be afraid, Mary, for you have found favor with God."

CA38 *The Annunciation by Lorenzo Monaco*

"And behold, you will conceive in your womb and bear a son, and you shall call his name Jesus."

"He will be great, and will be called the Son of the Most High..."

Lk 1:32   CA40   *The Annunciation by Master Bourbonnais of Moulins*

"...and the Lord God will give to him the throne of his father David..."

"...and he will reign over the house of Jacob for ever; and of his kingdom there will be no end."

The Annunciation in an Historical Initial R by Fra Angelico

And Mary said to the angel, "How can this be, since I have no husband?"

一九四八年春日太倉

陸鴻年敬繪於北平

And the angel said to her, "The Holy Spirit will come upon you, and the power of the Most High will overshadow you..."

Lk 1:35

CA44   Based on the Chinese scroll painting *The Annunciation to Mary* by John Lu Hung-nien

"...therefore the child to be born will be called holy, the Son of God."

"...your kinswoman Elizabeth in her old age
has also conceived a son; and this is the sixth
month with her who was called barren."

And Mary said, "Behold, I am the handmaid of the Lord; let it be to me according to your word."

And an angel of the Lord appeared to them, and the glory of the Lord shone around them...

Lk 2:9   CA48   *Angels Announce the Birth of Christ to the Shepherds by Carl Bloch*

Virgin and Child with Angels by Giovanni Del Ponte

CA49

Lk 2:11

"…for to you is born this day in the
city of David a Savior, who
is Christ the Lord."

...an angel of the Lord appeared to Joseph in a dream and said, "Rise, take the child and his mother, and flee to Egypt..."

CA50

Mt 2:13

Dream of Saint Joseph by Antonio Ciseri

Saint Joseph visited by an angel

"Rise, take the child and his mother, and go to the land of Israel, for those who sought the child's life are dead."

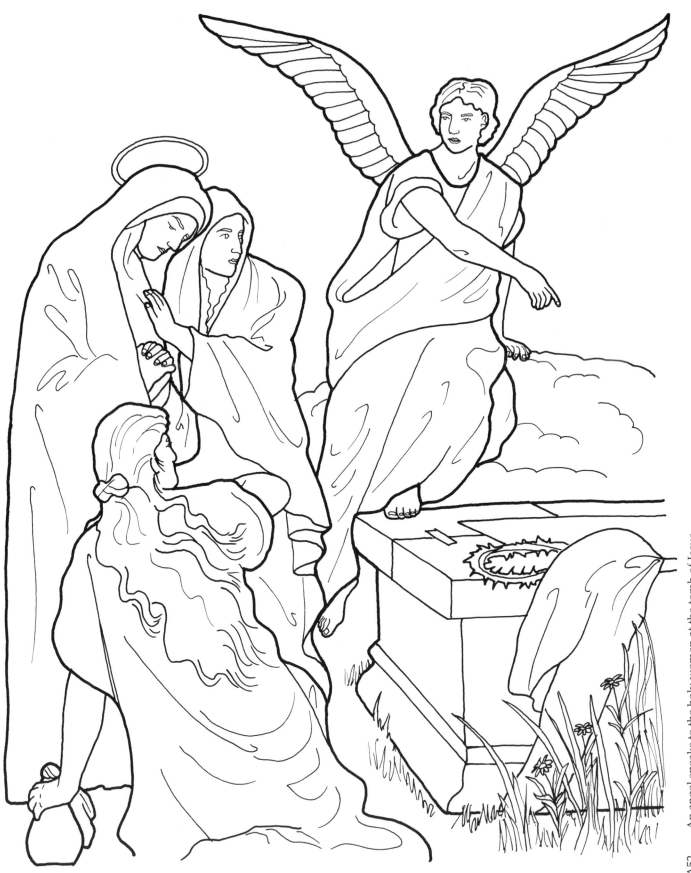

An angel speaks to the holy women at the tomb of Jesus

CA52

"He is not here; for he has risen, as he said. Come, see the place where he lay." Mt 28:6

Saint Matthew and the Angel by Michelangelo Merisi da Caravaggio

The book of the genealogy of
Jesus Christ, the son of David,
the son of Abraham.

"For I tell you that in heaven their angels always behold the face of my Father who is in heaven."

The Guardian Angel by Giovanni Francesco Barbieri

The Guardian Angel by Bartolomé Esteban Murillo

CA55

Ex 23:20

"Behold, I send an angel before you, to guard you on the way and to bring you to the place which I have prepared."

The angel of the Lord encamps around those who fear him, and delivers them.

Ps 34:7   CA56   *The Guardian Angel by Martin Feuerstein*

Guardian angel of the safe crossing

For he will give his angels charge
of you to guard you in all your ways.

"…make two cherubim of gold; of hammered work shall you make them, on the two ends of the mercy seat."

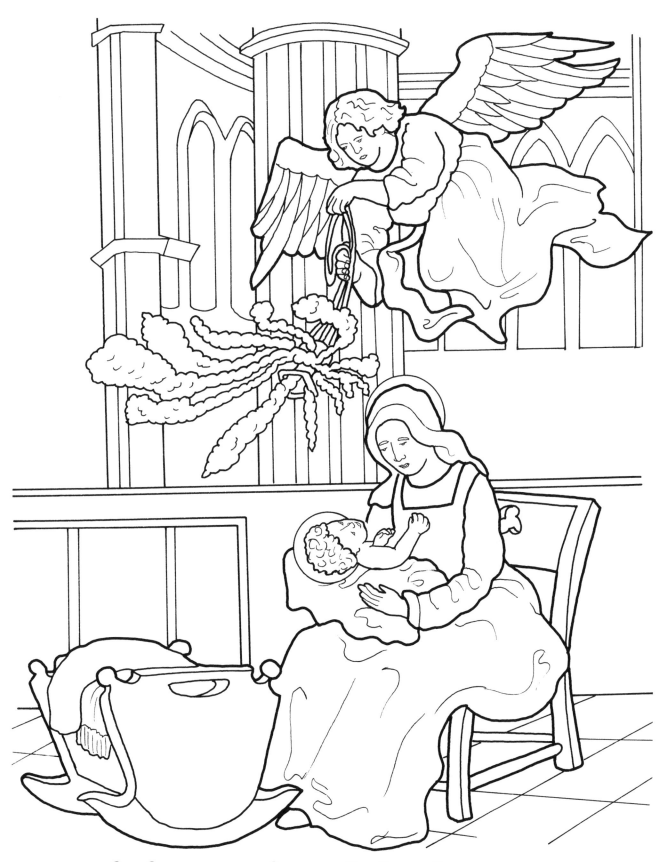

...and the smoke of the incense rose
with the prayers of the saints from the
hand of the angel before God.

...and I heard around the throne...the voice of many angels, numbering myriads of myriads...

Rev 5:11   CA60   *The Madonna in Majesty* (detail) by Bencivieni di Pepo (also known as Cimabue)

The Madonna in Majesty by Bencivieni di Pepo (also known as Cimabue)

Mt 25:31

"When the Son of man comes in his glory, and all the angels with him, then he will sit on his glorious throne."

And suddenly there was with the angel
a multitude of the heavenly host
praising God and saying...

The Virgin with Angels (detail) by William-Adolphe Bouguereau

CA62

"Glory to God in the highest, and on earth peace among men with whom he is pleased!"

He was manifested in the flesh,
vindicated in the Spirit,
seen by angels...

Sistine Madonna (angel detail) by Raphael Sanzio da Urbino

...preached among the nations,
believed on in the world,
taken up in glory.

But Mary kept all these things, pondering them in her heart.

CA66   *The Virgin and Child in Glory by Albrecht Altdorfer*

Madonna of the Canopy (angel detail) by Raphael Sanzio da Urbino

"But my lord has wisdom like the wisdom of the angel of God to know all things that are on the earth."

And one called to another and said:
"Holy, holy, holy is the Lord of hosts;
the whole earth is full of his glory."

The Virgin of Humility by Fra Angelico

...having become as much superior to angels as the name he has obtained is more excellent than theirs.

And again, when he brings the
firstborn into the world, he says,
"Let all God's angels worship him."

Saint Mary and the Choir of Angels from the Wilton Diptych

Madonna of the Cherubs by Giovanni Battista Salvi

Ez 10:19

And the cherubim lifted up their
wings and mounted up from the earth
in my sight as they went forth...

...you have come...to the city of the living God, the heavenly Jerusalem, and to innumerable angels in festal gathering...

CA72   *Immaculate Conception by José Claudio Antonlinez*   Heb 12:22